Edinburgh

Photographs by Colin Baxter
Introduction by Allan Massie
Text by Lorna Ewan

Colin Baxter Photography, Grantown-on-Spey, Scotland

Introduction

As capitals go, Edinburgh is still a small city. You can walk across it, south to north, in a couple of quite leisurely hours. (South to north is recommended, being mostly downhill.) The centre – the Old Town and the New Town, which latter is however two hundred years old – may be crossed in little more than a half-hour. Though the city, like most today, sometimes appears choked by the motor-car, it is a city where wheeled transport is unnecessary much of the time. Traditionally the Senators of the College of Justice, as Scotland's senior judges are splendidly known, and members of the Faculty of Advocates walk up the Mound from their residences in the New Town to Parliament House by the High Kirk of St Giles. Parliament House has been occupied by the lawyers since the Treaty of Union in 1707. The new Scottish Parliament found its first temporary home, further up the Royal Mile, in the Assembly Hall, which belongs to the Church of Scotland. Its permanent home since 2004 is in a new building at the other end of the Mile, by the gates of the royal Palace of Holyroodhouse.

Tourists throng the Royal Mile. It is one of the most remarkable streets in Europe. There are streets elsewhere with older buildings, but few retain their medieval quality as it does. It is in reality composed of three streets: the Lawnmarket at the top, the High Street in the middle, and the Canongate at the bottom. Actually, the Canongate was a separate burgh, outwith Edinburgh in the Middle Ages; and attached to the Abbey of the Holy Rood. 'Gate' incidentally means 'walk' – the Canons' walk – as in also the Cowgate which runs parallel to the Royal Mile, but at a lower level, and which leads to the Grassmarket below the Castle rock. The Scots word for a city gate was 'port', as in the West Port, at the western end of the Grassmarket.

The Castle, on its rock, overlooking the city, is the most famous and most immediately recognisable of the sights of Edinburgh. It is indeed so famous you might think it hackneyed. Yet it retains the power to surprise and impress. It is true that few of the buildings of which the Castle is composed – for it is not one building, but several – are, individually, very fine, though an exception must be made for Sir Robert Lorimer's Memorial to the dead of the 1914-18 war. The English travel writer H V Morton thought it 'the greatest war memorial in the world… The Flowers o' the Forest have

THE CITY FROM CALTON HILL (left)

all turned to stone…' But if, individually, the buildings are undistinguished, the total effect is magnificent, magnificently operatic. To attend the Tattoo on the Castle esplanade of a summer evening, and listen to the lone piper framed on the battlements is a thrilling experience, never forgotten, and one for which many return every year.

The Royal Mile is a street to be walked. You get a quite inadequate sense of it from a tourist bus. One reason is that to savour it fully, you must forever be making little diversions, into the closes and courts on either side of the street. These give you a keen sense of Old Edinburgh; they are picturesque and often of architectural interest; and they open to you surprising and delightful views of the sea or the hills beyond the city. For this is one of Edinburgh's features, remarked on lovingly by one of the city's most cherished sons, Robert Louis Stevenson: in no other city, he says, 'does the sight of the country enter so far… The place is full of theatre tricks in the way of scenery. You peep under an arch, you descend stairs that look as if they would land you in a cellar, you turn to the back window of a tenement in a grimy lane – and behold! You are face to face with distant and bright prospects. You turn a corner, and there is the sun going down into the Highland Hills. You look down an alley and see ships tacking for the Baltic…'

The ships today are more likely to be oil tankers heading to discharge their cargo at Grangemouth further up the Forth, but the surprise and delight remain. The city has grown since Stevenson's time, but the country still enters as he describes it. To front George Street on a clear bright morning and see the Firth of Forth below and beyond and the Lomond Hills of Fife on the further shore is to know the same exhilaration Stevenson knew.

Up till the second half of the eighteenth century, the Old Town was Edinburgh, with all sorts and conditions of people crowded together in the tall tenements. Below the Castle Rock, where Princes Street Gardens now are, was the Nor' Loch, and beyond that open country. There was no building on Calton Hill and the road to the Port of Leith ran between fields. But a more prosperous and self-consciously civilised age was demanding improvements, and the city was ready to escape its medieval bounds.

The first extension was indeed to the south, to George Square, whither Walter Scott's parents removed when he was still a small boy. George Square offered modest domestic architecture, agreeably proportioned, and made a harmonious whole until the University, in an act of vandalism, destroyed the south and east sides of the square in the 1960s. South of the High Street too, Robert Adam designed one of his masterpieces, now known as the Old College of the university.

But it was the building of the New Town that transformed Edinburgh. Inspired by Lord Provost

THE OLD TOWN, BALMORAL HOTEL AND CALTON HILL

Framed by the waters of the Firth of Forth the towers and chimneys of one of Edinburgh's eastern
skylines build an image of some of this city's many layers of history. There are the crow-stepped gables and astragal
windows of the tall Old Town tenements, the mid 19th-century, ornate turrets of the Church of Scotland's Assembly Hall,
the tiered structure of the Balmoral Hotel which was completed in 1902 and the monument to Lord Nelson
which pierces the skyline from the top of Calton Hill.

GEORGE STREET

The fine Georgian architecture of this street, itself named after King George III, is typical of the building forms and features found throughout Edinburgh's New Town. This area, from Princes Street to Queen Street, with George Street providing the main axis, was built between 1767 and 1800.

Drummond, the Nor' Loch was drained, and in 1763 the building of the North Bridge across the ravine was begun. A competition for the design of the bold development was won by a twenty-two-year-old architect named James Craig. What is called the first New Town, extending as far north as Queen Street, is essentially Craig's design, though the circus he planned for the middle of George Street, to complement the squares at either end, was never built. Work started at the east end, and evidence of confidence in Craig's plan was afforded by the construction of Register House, designed by the Adam brothers, Robert and James, to face up the North Bridge. It was funded incidentally by the Government from the sale of confiscated Jacobite estates.

The style of the New Town was carefully controlled by the imposition of strict feu conditions. The result is more apparent today in what came to be called the second New Town, built to the north and down the hill from the first. Commercial development has long ago destroyed the homogeneity of Princes Street and George Street, even of St Andrew Square, but in the second New Town, Heriot Row and Gillespie Graham's magnificent Moray Place provide evidence of what such control of individual whims and tastes could achieve.

The New Town had its critics from the first. Some deplored its uniformity, others, like Lord Cockburn, the loss of charming green countryside. A hundred years later, the art critic John Ruskin was still deploring its austere style: 'I cannot say it is entertaining,' he wrote. However Stevenson, born beyond the New Town in Howard Place but reared in Heriot Row, found it 'not only gay and airy, but picturesque'. On a fine day, Princes Street Gardens wore 'a surprising air of festival…It is what Paris ought to be.' He admitted however that 'the next morning the rain is splashing on the window, and the passengers flee along Princes Street before the galloping squalls.' Few have ever written with undiluted enthusiasm about Edinburgh's climate.

Another criticism was early directed at the New Town, and still surfaces today. The Old Town had been socially mixed. The New Town was not. Gradually the Old Town was abandoned to the poor, while the prosperous bourgeoisie ensconced themselves in the sedate squares and streets of the New. An American visitor remarked in 1834 that 'Paris is not more unlike Constantinople than one side of Edinburgh is unlike the other.'

Yet this contrast more than anything else has made the Edinburgh we know and have learned to love. The city is both classical and romantic, a double city, both open and secret. This was less obvious, or at least less pleasing, a hundred years ago than it is today, for then much of the Old Town had become a horrid slum, picturesque only to those who did not have to live there. Its renovation in the last fifty years has been remarkable, and it has been achieved without loss of its intrinsic character.

Naturally the city has continued to spread. There are

fine Victorian and Edwardian suburbs – no longer indeed to be classed as such – and both the nineteenth and twentieth centuries have seen much fine public building also. There is certainly a great deal to explore in Edinburgh beyond the Old and New Towns, as Colin Baxter's rich encyclopedia of photographs makes clear.

For all its beauty Edinburgh in the first half of the twentieth century could seem a dour, douce place. The poet Edwin Muir thought it a city that had lost, or forgotten, its reason for being. He could no longer say so. The catalyst for revival was the International Festival, that imaginative creation of three men: Henry Harvey Wood of the British Council, Rudolf Bing (conductor of the Glyndebourne Opera) and the Lord Provost, Sir John Falconer. It was conceived as a celebration of art and a restatement of the European ideal after the obscenity of Nazism. So Edinburgh lit a beacon in the cause of culture, amidst the miseries of post-war Europe, and culture, in the form of high art, gave new life to Edinburgh. The inauguration of the Festival in 1947 had a symbolic importance equal to that of the publication of Scott's *Waverley* in 1814.

Over the half-century since, Edinburgh has been transformed. It has re-invented itself and recovered its self-confidence. It has even, with the restoration of the Scottish Parliament, regained a political role it has been without since the Treaty of Union almost three hundred years ago.

In a world in which international styles of architecture often make one city so like another that a traveller suddenly woken from sleep would not know in which city, even which country, he found himself, Edinburgh, like Rome, remains distinctively itself. It is indeed unique; there is no city that much resembles it. Moreover it is still a city on a human scale, escaping the inhumanity which oppresses one in cities without its character. It is still intimate; even its National Galleries – the Portrait Gallery in Queen Street, the Gallery of Modern Art above the Dean Village, Playfair's National Gallery itself at the foot of the Mound – and the splendid new Museum of Scotland (an example of contemporary architecture at its best, original yet in accord with the mood of the city) – even all these Galleries then are of a size which is inviting rather than a deterrent.

The old name, the Athens of the North, is now meaningless. The real resemblance is to Rome, which offers the same delight to the eye and to the historical imagination. There is a saying that to know Rome 'one life is not enough'. It is true of Edinburgh also.

Allan Massie

DEACON BRODIE'S TAVERN (right) recalls William Brodie, respected councillor by day, infamous thief by night.

EDINBURGH MILITARY TATTOO AND THE CASTLE

Towering behind the crow-stepped frontages of the Grassmarket (right), the immense Castle walls dominate the city from almost every viewpoint. For some 7000 years people have lived on Castle Rock; here they built a fortress, a royal palace, a place of worship, a National War Memorial and today, the Castle is still home to the Scottish Crown Jewels and the Stone of Destiny. Since 1950, the world-famous Edinburgh Military Tattoo (left) has been performed nightly on the Castle Esplanade during the Edinburgh Festival.

THE SCOTT MONUMENT

Utterly different from any of the other architectural styles in Princes Street, the Scott Monument's gothic spire soars 200 feet above the street and stretches some 50 feet down to the bedrock below. The 64 statuettes which ornament the monument all represent characters from the novels of Sir Walter Scott, whose memory it honours as Scotland's most renowned romantic novelist. The centrepiece is a statue of Scott with his favourite dog, Maida. The monument was completed in 1846.

ARTHUR'S SEAT, SALISBURY CRAGS AND THE OLD TOWN

From the top of the Scott Monument, the view to the south-east reveals the medieval sprawl of the Old Town.
Towering above are the unmistakable tops of Arthur's Seat and Salisbury Crags. If more was needed to ensure Edinburgh's
uniqueness, these distinctive volcanic forms provide it. What other city in Britain can boast such a rugged open space?

PALACE OF HOLYROODHOUSE

Surmounted by the Royal Arms of Scotland, the grand entrance to Holyrood Palace forms the centrepiece of a range of buildings started in 1676. The tower-residence to the left was originally built for King James V between 1529 and 1532.

PALACE OF HOLYROODHOUSE FROM SALISBURY CRAGS

Behind Holyrood Palace nestle the ruins of Holyrood's medieval Abbey, of which Mendelssohn said 'I believe I found the beginning of my Scottish symphony here.' Founded in 1128 by King David I, the Abbey probably took its name from a relic thought to be part of Christ's *rood* or cross. As a royal residence the Palace of Holyrood is one of the most ancient places still used by the royal family. Successive monarchs used the Abbey's guest houses and gradually it became an important domicile with the first elements of today's great quadrangular palace being started in the early 16th century.

VICTORIA STREET

Built between 1829 and 1834, this is one of the most characterful streets in Edinburgh. It could only be constructed after the building of George IV Bridge to which it is joined at its upper end. Unusually, and often to the confusion of visitors, the bottom half of what is apparently the same street is called the West Bow. Used since at least the 12th century, the bow or gate originally turned sharply up towards the Castle, before the road was extended by the building of Victoria Street, with its round-arched shop windows and the curving Victoria Terrace which surmounts it.

ST GILES' SPIRE AND THE OLD TOWN AT DUSK

In the gentle dusk light it seems unlikely that violence could erupt in St Giles', the High Kirk of Edinburgh. However, the story goes that in 1637 when the authorities tried to introduce the English Prayer Book, and in turn Episcopal government, one local stallholder was so incensed that she hurled her stool at the unsuspecting preacher, so prompting the rest of the congregation to chase him from the building.

THE CASTLE, RAMSAY GARDEN AND THE NATIONAL GALLERY

Every year, after the Festival-goers have left, Edinburgh almost seems to stop and catch
its breath, as it recovers from the heady energy of the previous weeks. Snow is unusual in the city
centre, but adds an air of tranquillity to this winter scene.

BALMORAL HOTEL AND NORTH BRIDGE

North Bridge was the essential link from the Old Town across to the open fields where the vision of
the New Town awaited. The first bridge took 11 years to build after the foundation stone was laid in 1763.
At the end of the 19th century the present bridge was built to accommodate the railway station below.

CHARLOTTE SQUARE

Charlotte Square's unusual octagonal gardens now provide a home to the Edinburgh Book Festival every August.
This popular tented event is watched over by a bronze equestrian statue of Prince Albert in the centre of the gardens.

RAMSAY GARDEN AND THE OUTLOOK TOWER

Largely designed by town-planner Patrick Geddes in the 'organic and improvisatory' style, this fascinating amalgam includes the earlier Outlook Tower, once an observatory, but later fitted out by Geddes himself as the world's first 'sociological laboratory'.

THE CITY FROM SALISBURY CRAGS (left)

THE HIGH STREET AT FESTIVAL TIME

Every August, Edinburgh is almost overwhelmed with atmosphere as people flock to the city for the
International Festival of Music and Drama. The first major post-war festival of arts in Europe, it began in August 1947.

FESTIVAL FRINGE OFFICE, ROYAL MILE

Now an Edinburgh institution in itself, the Fringe was an informal by-product of the first Edinburgh Festival when eight theatre groups simply arrived and contributed. Today the office in the High Street (part of the Royal Mile) is at the heart of this event, for which about half a million tickets are sold for around 10,000 performances in over 150 venues every year. For over half a century the Fringe has continued its spontaneous evolution.

FESTIVAL FIREWORKS

In recent years the Fireworks Concert has become one of the biggest events of the Edinburgh Festival. With the Scottish Chamber Orchestra playing in the Ross Bandstand of Princes Street Gardens, and a choreographed display of magnificent pyrotechnics exploding from the Castle walls, people crowd into the city centre in their thousands. Every space is filled with radio-carrying spectators as picnickers line the edge of Salisbury Crags and revellers vie for a place to sit on the top of Calton Hill.

OLD TOWN SKYLINE AGAINST SALISBURY CRAGS

In the 16th century over 700 people lived above each acre of land in the Old Town. Above,
because their homes were the 'teeming, tottering' tenements graded socially from the highest floor to the
deepest basement. About half of the Old Town was demolished during 19th-century improvements.

THE CASTLE AND BANK OF SCOTLAND DOME

The geometric lines of the Castle provide a stunning backdrop to the ornate Roman Baroque
architecture of the Bank of Scotland's head office. A gilded statue depicting 'Fame' crowns the great dome.

BALMORAL HOTEL CLOCK TOWER AND CITY SPIRES

Edinburgh, the 'City of Spires'. The remarkable stylistic variety of the soaring structures which so characterise the skyline, can no better be described than in the contrast between the massive, square clock tower of the Balmoral Hotel, the fragile turrets of the Scott Monument, and, in the distance, two of the three Victorian Gothic spires of St Mary's Cathedral at the West End.

HERIOT ROW, NEW TOWN (left)

When the grand homes of the New Town were built, though considerably better than accommodation in the Old Town, they were still damp, had no baths and 'the conveniences were few in number'. Fortunately, times have changed and the elegant facades now house some of Edinburgh's most gracious residences.

MORAY PLACE, NEW TOWN (right)

Moray Place forms the core of the most complex New Town development, the Moray Estate, built in the first half of the 19th century.

THE FORTH RAIL BRIDGE

The three massive steel cantilever structures give the Forth Rail Bridge its unmistakable and universally recognised identity. During its construction between 1883 and 1890, 57 men lost their lives and eight million rivets were hammered into place to hold the 55,000 tons of steel together. Today the bridge is a world-famous testament to Scottish engineering.

GEORGE HERIOT'S SCHOOL

This fine Renaissance building was completed in about 1700. The consequence of a bequest of £23,625 from the goldsmith George Heriot, it was founded as a 'hospital' for the education of orphaned boys. Known as 'Jinglin' Geordie', Heriot was banker to Anne of Denmark and then to her husband King James VI.

GLADSTONE'S LAND

This remarkable Old Town survivor is now
furnished as a 17th-century merchant's
house. The building, which incorporates
a 16th-century tenement and contains
mortar from an even earlier date, has the
only remaining arcaded street frontage
which was once the official standard for
the Old Town. In 1935, its facade hidden
behind later works, Gladstone's Land was
condemned by the city. Fortunately the
owner donated the 'Land' to the National
Trust for Scotland who discovered the
original exterior during restoration.

CANONGATE KIRK (left)

In 1691, the architecturally unique Canongate Kirk replaced Holyrood Abbey as the local parish church. On its gable are the Royal Arms of King William III. The antlers commemorate a medieval legend about the founding of Holyrood Abbey in the 12th century, when, following an attack on King David I by an enraged stag, a cross miraculously appeared between its antlers. A dominant building in the Canongate, the Kirk is flanked by the many 'closes' or alleyways which lead off the Royal Mile.

WHITEHORSE CLOSE (right)

Originally built in the 17th century, this picturesque close was restored in 1889 and again in 1962, when modern building techniques were hidden by traditional harling. The first Edinburgh–London stagecoach left the White Horse Inn here in 1749.

THE OLD TOWN

Founded around 1140 by King David I, the Old Town of Edinburgh was described in the
15th century as the 'capital of Scotland where the king chiefly resides when he is in that part of the country.'

EDINBURGH CASTLE, PRINCES STREET AND PRINCES STREET GARDENS

In 1816 an Act of Parliament secured the future of Princes Street Gardens by ensuring
that no building would occur on the south side of Princes Street. Initially the Gardens were exclusive to
Princes Street proprietors as a place to promenade; where gentlemen were not permitted to smoke pipes but only cigars.
Gradually the Gardens became more widely accessible at first at Christmas and New Year only,
but by 1876 they had become Edinburgh's best-known public gardens.

FETTES COLLEGE FROM THE QUEENSFERRY ROAD

Fettes College completely dominates the skyline of the flat, low-lying area of Inverleith. Described as a Scottish baronial-French Gothic masterpiece, the school was founded using funds left by the tea and wine merchant Sir William Fettes, twice provost of the city. The boarding school was designed by David Bryce, architect of over 100 country houses and 'inventor' of the Scottish baronial style.

DEAN VILLAGE (right)

Edinburgh's largest milling settlement was originally called 'Water of Leith Village', from the river which supplied its power.

ROYAL MUSEUM OF SCOTLAND AND McEWAN HALL (left)

New and old tower in dramatic contrast. The smooth curving lines of the Museum of Scotland stand as a monument to late 20th-century architecture, as the low dome and lantern apex of the McEwan Hall stand for building design 100 years earlier.

ST GILES' CATHEDRAL AND THE ROYAL MILE (right)

St Giles' Cathedral, the High Kirk of Edinburgh, proudly rises through a confusion of architectural styles, from four Norman columns to the mid 16th-century golden weathercock, pinnacle of the famous crown spire.

BALMORAL HOTEL, CLOCK TOWER

Some 190 feet high, the massive form of the Balmoral Hotel clock tower is one of the most familiar features of the Edinburgh skyline. Dominating the east end of Princes Street the clock has, for generations, ensured that harassed travellers catch their trains in Waverley Station far below, by being just a minute or two fast! The hotel itself was the pride of the Edwardian North British Railway Company.

THE BALMORAL HOTEL, SOUTH FACE

Originally called the North British, the hotel, with its extravagant bows and balconies, was constructed
as part of the building of the North Bridge which joins the Old Town to the New. It was completed in 1902.

THE CASTLE AND CITY AT DUSK FROM CALTON HILL

The line cleaving Edinburgh in two is still sharply defined today. To the south is the tangle of the Old Town,
to the north, the classical lines of the New. The former a medieval capital, once overcrowded and disease-ridden,
is now charming and impressive by turn. The latter is a city built on the vision of men like George Drummond, six times
provost of the city, who in 1752 stated that it 'should naturally become the centre of trade and commerce, of learning
and the arts, of politeness, and of refinement of every kind'. A century later the vision was complete.

INDIA STREET, NEW TOWN

India Street, like nearby Jamaica Street, was named after the then British colony. These streets formed part of the Northern or Second New Town development which was planned in the first two years of the 19th century. Lying on a north-facing slope overlooking the Firth of Forth, this scheme was by far the largest of the New Town developments. India Street is unusual insofar as it contains houses as well as main-door tenement buildings.

RAMSAY GARDEN

In 1887 Patrick Geddes established the first student residence in Scotland, on the Mound. During the next decade he conceived the Ramsay Garden buildings as his 'University Hall Extension' which was a Town-and-Gown hall of residence and a block of flats. Clinging to their steep, sloping site the buildings incorporated the pre-existing Ramsay Lodge and three other mid 18th-century houses.

RAMSAY GARDEN FROM THE CASTLE ESPLANADE

Today, the highly desirable flats of Ramsay Garden command panoramic
views northward over the city, and exclusive views of the Castle to the west.

FORTH ROAD BRIDGE

When the Bridge opened in 1964 it was the longest suspension bridge in Europe. Prior to its opening,
the usual way to cross the Firth of Forth was to take the Queen's Ferry. Over the centuries others found different
ways of crossing; Vincent Lunardi used a balloon, William Wallace swam, and King Edward I of England
intended to use pre-fabricated bridges brought by sea from Norfolk.

TOWARDS THE CALEDONIAN HOTEL FROM THE MOUND

Although technically at the bottom of Lothian Road, the enormous tiers of red sandstone which are the
Caledonian Hotel truly punctuate the west end of Princes Street. Originally designed as an entrance to the station in
1890-93, the V-shaped hotel held the train shed between its two massive arms until the station closed in 1965.

OLD TOWN ROOFTOPS
AND CALTON HILL FROM
THE OUTLOOK TOWER (left)

The confusion of buildings that is Edinburgh's Old Town was once the most overcrowded city in Europe.

MYLNE'S COURT,
OLD TOWN (right)

In 1750, only 60 years after this 'close' was built, there were some 200 closes and wynds running out from the Royal Mile, the spine of the Old Town. This one was constructed by Robert Mylne of Balfarg, 7th Royal Master Mason. Only about 100 of the old closes survive but their atmosphere now, so different from the cramped, soiled conditions of times past, is pleasant and often unexpected.

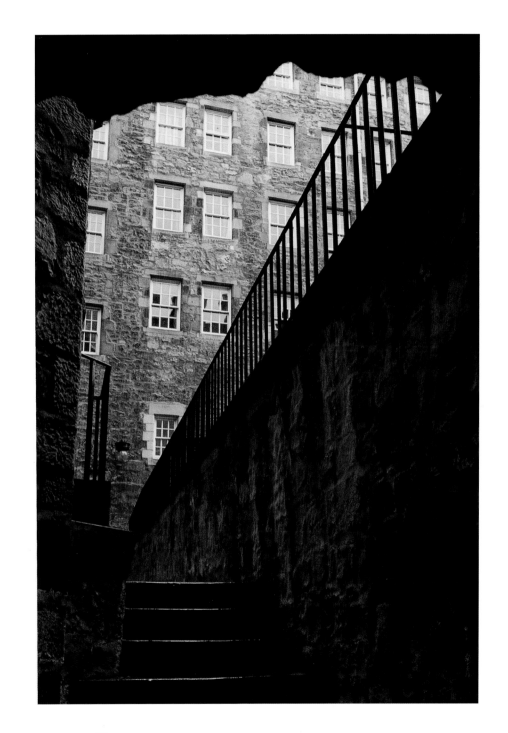

RAMSAY GARDEN
IN SPRINGTIME (left)

The name derives from that of Allan Ramsay, the early 18th-century poet who began his working life as a wig-maker and whose statue stands in Princes Street Gardens. He is remembered for his work 'The Gentle Shepherd' and for the eccentric design of Ramsay Lodge in the middle of Ramsay Garden. The octagonal house was built in about 1740 as a place where he could 'be away from the clatter of the High Street'.

CASTLE AND CITY
AT TWILIGHT (right)

BANK OF SCOTLAND AND ASSEMBLY HALL
A south-eastern view over Princes Street Gardens, to the familiar skyline of the Old Town.

PRINCES STREET AND SPIRES AT DUSK (left)

THE MEADOWS AND MARCHMONT

Once the waters of the Burgh Loch, the green expanse of the Meadows was reclaimed between 1722 and 1740. Late in 1873 some young men, who were soon to call themselves Heart of Mid-Lothian, played their first game of 'football' (then a mixture of soccer and rugby) there. By the end of the decade the Meadows were home to over a dozen clubs who played each Saturday in front of hundreds of spectators and 'Hearts' were well on the way to establishing themselves as one of Edinburgh's predominant teams.

THE NELSON MONUMENT AND ST ANDREW'S HOUSE

The Monument to Lord Nelson was intended as a place of residence for 'a few disabled seamen'. How the disabled tenants were expected to reach their rooms is not clear but the space was in any case 'leased to a vendor of soups and sweetmeats'. At the top a zinc-plated wooden time ball 5' 6" in diameter provided a visual signal to ships on the Forth enabling them to set their chronometers at precisely 1pm. St Andrew's House, in the foreground, was built as governmental offices in the 1930s.

SCOTT MONUMENT AT DUSK

Whether by whimsy, ignorance or good judgement, Edinburgh Council selected a carpenter to design the Scott Monument at a time when the city was oozing with talented architects. Perhaps his was simply the best design. George Kemp certainly oversaw the construction for most of the six years it took to build (1840-46). But Kemp never saw his edifice completed; on his way home one night he fell into the Union Canal and drowned.

CASTLE AND OLD TOWN AT DUSK
The Castle Esplanade, Castlehill, the Lawnmarket, High Street, Netherbow, Canongate and Abbey Strand
stretch down the hill between the Castle drawbridge and the gates of Holyrood Palace to form the Royal Mile.

ASSEMBLY HALL, OUTLOOK TOWER AND THE PENTLAND HILLS

The Outlook Tower was extended upwards in the 1850s to allow for the installation of the Camera Obscura on the top.

ARTHUR'S SEAT AND THE MEADOWS (right)

NATIONAL GALLERY AND SPIRES

The classical exterior of the National Gallery houses the most important collection of Old Masters in Britain, outside London. In recent years the Gallery's interiors were redecorated and the paintings and sculptures redisplayed in an attempt to return the rooms to the 1840s style as designed by William Playfair.

NORTH BRIDGE, OLD TOWN BUILDINGS AND CASTLE (left)

WEST BOW AND GRASSMARKET

For many centuries the Grassmarket was the site of both the corn and livestock markets for the city.
Here also, at the foot of the West Bow, was the site of the town gibbet. Marked now by the Covenanters' Memorial,
erected in 1937, this place commemorates the martyrdom of all those who died here for their beliefs.

GREYFRIARS BOBBY

Thanks to the power of Hollywood this Skye terrier is known the world over. He was probably a police dog working with a constable called John Gray who died in 1858. When Gray was buried in the Greyfriars Kirkyard, Bobby began a vigil on the grave which lasted until his death 14 years later. Local people fed and cared for the dog, even providing him with a collar to prevent him being impounded as a stray. This commemorative statue stands on a street corner just near the kirkyard off George IV Bridge.

THE CASTLE AND PRINCES STREET GARDENS

John Buchan claimed that more history had been made in Edinburgh than in any place of similar size, with the possible exceptions of Athens, Rome and Jerusalem. In the Castle alone: the Scottish Crown Jewels, the oldest in western Europe, were lost for 111 years, and Mary, Queen of Scots gave birth to a child who would become the first monarch of Scotland and England after the Union of the Crowns in 1603.

CHARLOTTE SQUARE, EAST SIDE

Designed by Robert Adam, Charlotte Square is for many the zenith of New Town architecture. Professor Joseph Lister, who famously developed antiseptic surgery, was one of many doctors and lawyers who chose to live in this elegant square.

OLD TOWN AND ST GILES' CATHEDRAL

Edinburgh's medieval Old Town was only about a mile in length by 1000 feet wide,
yet this was the full extent of the twin burghs of Edinburgh and Canongate for some 650 years.

BIBLE LAND, CANONGATE

Fine stone carving embellishes many doors
and closes in the Old Town. The crafted
lines of the masons' work sit clearly
against the textured rubble-built walls
of the older buildings. The Bible Land
double tenement has been almost
entirely rebuilt since it was erected
by the Incorporation of Cordiners
(or Shoemakers) in 1677. The cartouche
above the door carries the 'Cordiners'
emblem of the crowned shoemaker's
rounding knife flanked by cherubs' heads'.

CANONGATE TOLBOOTH

Dating from the late 16th century, this landmark building was once the town hall for the independent burgh of Canongate. Despite its close proximity to Edinburgh, the Canongate, or 'road of the canons', existed as a separate town until 1856. Today, the building serves as a museum telling 'The People's Story'.

NATIONAL GALLERY OF SCOTLAND

The Ionic columns of the neoclassical National Gallery were part of the design produced by William
Playfair between 1850 and 1854. He was also responsible for designing the Royal Scottish Academy whose grand classical
lines stand in a magnificent twinning with the National Gallery at the bottom of the Mound.

THE CASTLE AND PRINCES STREET GARDENS IN AUTUMN

Princes Street Gardens now flourish where the Nor' Loch, a defensive artificial loch, was created in 1460. Over time the Loch became brackish and polluted by the butchers and tanners who worked on its banks. Before it was drained it was described as 'a fetid and festering marsh, the receptacle for skinned horses, drowned dogs, frogs and worried cats.'

THE CASTLE, RAMSAY GARDEN AND ASSEMBLY HALL

The stark Tudor facade of the Assembly Hall, the clustered forms of Ramsay
Garden and the massive stone edifice of the Castle sit together in remarkable harmony.

JOHN KNOX HOUSE, ROYAL MILE

It is unlikely that John Knox ever stayed in this 16th-century house, but the legend which associates him with the building probably ensured its survival in the Old Town High Street. Knox himself, though never more than a preacher, was the key figure in the Scottish Reformation which saw Protestant revolt against Papal power and theology. The coat of arms on the front are those of James Mossman, goldsmith, and his wife Mariota Arres, who lived here in the 16th century.

CHRISTMAS TREE
ON THE MOUND

In every season the sweeping
curve of the Mound is impressive.
Its construction, required to join the
New to the Old Town about halfway
along Princes Street, was the result of
commercial imperative. As professionals
moved to the New Town, existing
businesses in the Old Town lost customers.
To improve access, the Mound was built,
first as a causeway of stones and debris;
eventually its mass was formed by an
estimated 1,300,000 cartloads of earth.

THE CITY AT DUSK FROM CALTON HILL

Every year the lights of the Mound Christmas tree shine brightly across Princes Street and the city centre.
James Craig, whose plans won the competition for the design of the New Town in 1767, conceived Princes Street to have a
panoramic view of the Castle and Old Town; fortunately no building has since been allowed to despoil that principle.

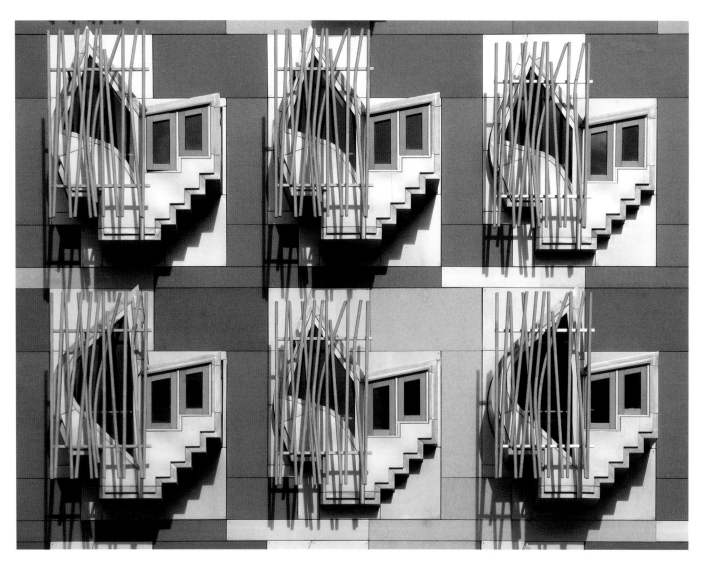

THE SCOTTISH PARLIAMENT, HOLYROOD

The new home of the Scottish Parliament (MSP's office windows *above*, and from the air *opposite*) was officially opened in 2004. The Catalan architect Enric Miralles drew inspiration for the building's innovative design from the surrounding landscape, and from upturned boats for the roofs. It has won a number of architectural awards.

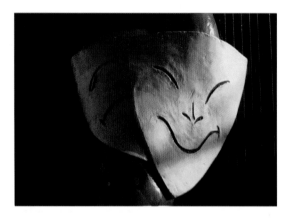

THE PEOPLE'S STORY, CANONGATE

FESTIVAL FRINGE OFFICE

CASTLEHILL

ROYAL MILE DETAIL

MOUBRAY HOUSE

WILLIAM 'DEACON' BRODIE

LAWNMARKET

CANONGATE

THE HEART OF MIDLOTHIAN

THE ROYAL MILE AND ST GILES' CATHEDRAL

So often it is scale or beauty which grabs the attention, like the grand structure of St Giles' Cathedral, a place of worship and learning. But just down the hill in Anchor Close a printer and an engraver once conceived an idea for a new, weekly publication. The first edition, price 6d, hit the streets in December 1768. Now available to anyone on-line, it was the *Encyclopaedia Britannica*; its foundation is commemorated by a small rusty plaque.

THE CASTLE AND RAMSAY GARDEN

Looking at the attractive shapes of Ramsay Garden and the Castle, it is hard to imagine that over the years more than 300 women were burned to death on a spot just between the two, near the foot of the Esplanade. Today an elegant Art Nouveau fountain marks the place, the Witches' Fountain, where the women accused of witchcraft and sorcery died such dreadful deaths. The last burning was in 1722.

FOOG'S GATE, EDINBURGH CASTLE

The 17th-century Foog's Gate frames what is now the main entrance to the enclosed royal citadel
on the summit of Castle Rock. Previously the steep Lang Stairs were the principal access to the summit where
St Margaret's Chapel, the oldest part of the Castle, stands on the highest point of the Rock.

LEITH WATERFRONT

Vibrant and energetic, the waterfront restaurants and pubs of Leith have brought a new atmosphere to this redeveloped area.

SHIP SIGN, LEITH (right)

THE OLD TOWN FROM THE NEW TOWN

THE MEADOWS, OLD ROYAL INFIRMARY AND UNIVERSITY

Above the trees, the Scottish baronial towers of the Old Royal Infirmary contrast with the
modern concrete forms of the University's Appleton Tower and Library. Built between 1872 and 1879,
the Infirmary replaced the earlier hospital on the congested Old Town site in Infirmary Street.
The new Royal Infirmary, built at Little France, south-east Edinburgh, opened in 2003.

OLD TOWN CHIMNEYS

No wonder Edinburgh was nicknamed 'auld reekie'. Smoke from thousands of chimneys, mingled with the unpleasant odours and effluents from the many mills and breweries, ensured that for decade upon decade the people of Edinburgh rarely saw a blue sky or breathed fresh air. Today smokeless zone regulations ensure clear views across the city.

THE CITY FROM SALISBURY CRAGS

From this vantage point the spires and towers of the city rise clearly above the rooftops,
which extend to a horizon now far beyond just the Old and New Towns at the city's contrasting core.

RAMSAY GARDEN IN WINTER
Winter snow confers an unfamiliar look to this fairy-tale
collection of houses, which date mainly from the 18th and 19th centuries.

SCOTT MONUMENT
AND THE CLASSIC TOUR

Whatever the season, Edinburgh always welcomes visitors to explore its many spires and monuments. The list is practically infinite: the ornate pinnacle to Sir Walter Scott, the Regimental Memorials in Princes Street Gardens or the National War Memorial in the Castle itself. But beyond these are hundreds, perhaps thousands of other memorials to the writers and artists from Robert Burns to Sir Henry Raeburn, to the scientists and engineers, to architects and to doctors from Elsie Inglis to Joseph Lister, all of whom have lived and worked in this city.

NO. 6 CHARLOTTE SQUARE (left)

Bute House, or number 6 Charlotte Square, was the official residence of the Secretary of State for Scotland, chosen by the government in preference to Edinburgh Castle. Since the establishment of the Scottish Parliament in 1999 it is now the official residence of the First Minister. On the top level in number 7 is the official residence of the Moderator of the Church of Scotland, with the National Trust's Georgian House filling the remainder of the building.

THE CASTLE AND BALMORAL HOTEL (right)

The Castle in twilight assumes a regal air high on Castle Rock, and overlooks a city of many splendours.

Index of Places

Arthur's Seat — 13, 63
Assembly Hall — 57, 62, 75
Balmoral Hotel — 5, 20, 29, 44, 45, 95
Bank of Scotland — 28, 57
Caledonian Hotel — 51
Calton Hill — 2, 5, 52, 59
Canongate — 36, 71, 72, 82
Castle — front cover 1, 10, 11, 19, 22, 26, 28, 39, 46, 55, 61, 64, 68, 74, 75, 79, 84, 85, 91, 95
Castlehill — 82, 88
Charlotte Square — 21, 69, 94
Deacon Brodie's Tavern — 9
Dean Village — 41
Festival Fireworks — 26
Festival Fringe Office — 25, 82
Fettes College — 40
Forth, Firth of — 5
Forth Rail Bridge — 32, 33
Forth Road Bridge — 50
George Heriot's School — 34
George Street — 6
Gladstone's Land — 35
Grassmarket — 11, 66
Greyfriars Bobby — 67
Heart of Midlothian — 82
Heriot Row — 30
India Street — 47
John Knox House — 76, 77
Lawnmarket — 9, 82
Leith — 86, 87
Marchmont — 58
McEwan Hall Spire — 42

Meadows, The — 58, 63, 89
Military Tattoo — 10
Mylne's Court — 53
Moray Place — 31
Moubray House — 82
Mound — 57
National Gallery of Scotland — 19, 65, 73
Nelson Monument — 5, 59
New Town — 30, 31, 46
North Bridge — 20, 64
Old Royal Infirmary — 89
Old Town — 5, 13, 18, 27, 35, 38, 46, 52, 53, 61, 64, 70, 90, back cover
Outlook Tower — 23, 62
Palace of Holyroodhouse — 14, 15
Pentland Hills — 62
People's Story — 82
Princes Street — 12, 39, 51, 56, 96
Princes Street Gardens — 19, 39, 57, 68, 74
Ramsay Garden — 19, 23, 48, 49, 54, 75, 84, 92
Royal Mile — 9, 24, 25, 43, 76, 82, 83
Royal Museum of Scotland — 42
Royal Scottish Academy — 88
Salisbury Crags — 13, 27
Scott Monument — 12, 29, 60, 93
Scottish Parliament — 80, 81
St Giles' Cathedral — 18, 22, 43, 70, 83, back cover
St Mary's Cathedral — 29
University of Edinburgh — 42, 89
Victoria Street — 16, 17
West Bow — 66
Whitehorse Close — 37

Revised and updated paperback edition first
published by Colin Baxter Photography Ltd in 2006.

First published in Great Britain in 2000 by
Lomond Books.   Reprinted 2003.

Produced by Colin Baxter Photography Ltd.
Photographs Copyright © Colin Baxter 2006.
Text Copyright © Colin Baxter Photography Ltd 2006.
www.colinbaxter.co.uk

ISBN 1-84107-316-4   978-184107-316-3   Printed in China

Front Cover Photograph: Edinburgh Castle and Balmoral Hotel   **Page 1 Photograph:** City Skyline at Dusk   **Back Cover Photograph:** The Old Town